# Contents

# LOVE, LEADERSHIP, *and* LOYALTY

## What It Takes to Be the BEST BOSS Ever

### DR. KAREN M. WALKER

Industrial / Organizational Psychologist
Lieutenant Colonel, USMC (ret.)

**KW Productions**

*Published by:*
**KW Productions**
GERMANTOWN, MARYLAND

ISBN: 978-0-578-62578-2

Editing: KW Productions

Cover and interior: Gary A. Rosenberg
www.thebookcouple.com

Printed in the United States of America

# Acknowledgments

I want to give a special thank you to my family and friends for your constant encouragement to keep challenging the status quo. Also, thank you to all those who came before me and weathered the storms of resentment and persecution for being better than the rest. This book is for the pursuit of equality and making our world a better place for our future. Praise to God. May we be given all that we choose to give in life. Love, leadership, and loyalty. Ductus Exemplo.

# Foreword

I HAVE OFTEN BEEN THE ONLY GIRL on the field ever since I can remember. Like my brother, I played baseball. Unlike my brother, I was told I should quit baseball. Why? Because I'm a girl. I was always better than my brother but because I was a girl, certain coaches wanted me to quit the game I loved. This gender discrimination didn't make any sense to me so I decided that no matter what came my way, I wouldn't quit on my baseball dreams.

When I was 16, I decided I wanted to become a college baseball coach. At the time no woman had coached at the college level. I was a shy teenager and had not shared my dream with anyone. I decided to tell my coach about my dream. His response? He laughed at me and claimed, "no man will listen to a woman on a baseball field." I was crushed and embarrassed. But as I began to think about it. I thought, who is he to limit what I can do.

Almost 20 years later, I was the only woman college baseball coach in the country. And what I learned is that most players don't care about my gender. What they did care about was whether I knew what I was talking about, did I care about them as people and whether I could make them a better player. During those same college years, I became the first woman to coach pro baseball (Brockton Rox, CanAm League, 2009).

Not everyone on the pro team was on board with having a female coach on the team. I was told by a fellow older coach that I was useless and that he didn't want me on his field. He claimed, "I was a nice doll and all, but he can go to any bar and get a doll."

Similar to when I was 16 years old and told I could never be a baseball coach, I had to decide what my next action would be. I decided I would be kind when others were mean. I couldn't let the chaos of anger lead me. I needed to keep my own peace. So I decided on kindness. When I was kicked out of the locker room, my daughter, Jasmine, and I made the team brownies.

I was going to be kind but I was not going to allow people to ignore me. I staged my own silent protest. After each game, I quickly walked back to the locker room entrance and took a seat near the door. This way the whole team had to walk by me as the game ended and they went to change their clothes and eat dinner. Dinner was only served inside the lockerroom.

One evening, as I sat waiting outside the lockerroom, the equipment manager brought me some food. I began eating alone. Then one evening while I ate alone, the door opened and our catcher came out with his dinner and sat next to me. When the catcher left, another player came out and sat with me and ate. I don't know what we talked about but their actions showed me that I was not alone in my journey.

I believe those players sat with me because I chose kindness over anger. I led with courage, vulnerability, and resilience. I had earned their respect. Respect I don't think I would have received if I had reacted poorly to the insults, slights, and difficulties.

In "Love, Leadership, and Loyalty," Dr. Walker shows us that leadership is not about coercion but about care, understanding, and action. Whether it's baseball players or soldiers, the best boss we can have is the one who shows us how we can be our best selves.

You know that coach who told me I was useless and compared me to a "doll?" Six years later, he recommended me for a coaching job! I had won him over. As you read through Dr. Walker's meaningful and pertinent words, remember that whatever obstacles are placed in front of you, lead with your heart, with kindness, and a resilience to go after your dreams.

Dr. Justine Siegal

*First woman to coach for a MLB organization*

*First woman to throw batting practice to an MLB team*

*Founder & Director of Baseball for All, a nonprofit organization that provides meaningful opportunities and instruction in baseball, especially for girls*

## PRELUDE

# From a Lady in Uniform

**MY NAME IS DR. KAREN WALKER,** Lieutenant Colonel (Retired). I am fortunate to have successfully completed three combat tours in support of Operation Iraqi Freedom, and I am thankful to continue to live each day as a dream that writes itself. After everything I have accomplished and been through in my life, my number one mantra for working with others is still: "I am not in competition with you. I am NOT your competition. I am your biggest advocate and ally, and I need you to be mine."

The purpose of *Love, Leadership, Loyalty: What it Takes to Be the Best Boss Ever*, is to share the raw power that comes from the vulnerability of being a leader. This book provides highlights from the hundreds of interviews, assessments, and experiences I have gathered as an human behavior practitioner and research psychologist. As a civilian, I am an industrial/organizational psychologist with a passion for sparking change through advocacy. I have studied leadership from all angles, but most vividly through the measurement of behaviors and critical incidents that have defined people's "best" and "worst" bosses. By sharing these real experiences in the truest form, I hope that others' lives will be touched and transformed. Through this fearless collaboration, leaders of all stripes will know they are not alone, from the top of the organization down to the new graduates about to embark on their careers.

I share my truth openly and vulnerably. Vulnerability is a key aspect of leadership as it allows people to see the human element of the leader. As children, we learn valuable skills from what we observe. As adults, we learn valuable skills from not only what we observe but from what we put into practice.

What are you practicing? If you want to be more trustworthy, you must live, breathe, and do it every single day. Being vulnerable is uncomfortable and it's something that takes practice. It means we have to be open and honest with ourselves and others. When you master vulnerability in a position of leadership, you increase your power to communicate, collaborate, and, most importantly, connect with people. Vulnerability is the key to building long-lasting and *trusting* relationships, whether they are personal or professional.

My recommendation is that you take the time to invest in yourself and measure where you are, so you know where you need the most development. Then you can focus on specific areas for improvement. It takes practice to make change happen, and when people see you putting in a consistent effort, they will know you are walking the talk. Behavioral change comes with consistent measurement of goals and objectives.

Let's get started in finding out *what it takes to be the best boss ever* by first looking into who you truly are. It's going to take hard work and a battle mindset. It's what I like to call: Combat Pink! Join me and take the opportunity to practice each behavior along the way. Most importantly, don't forget to measure where you are because:

*"What gets measured is what gets done!"*

# CHAPTER 1

# Combat Pink–Who Am I?

SO MUCH OF LIFE IS ABOUT DISCOVERY. As a psychologist, I am asked if I can read minds. Sometimes I tell people "yes" just to freak them out. The truth, however, is that I am an expert in human behavior and I specialize in people at work as an industrial/organizational psychologist. As humans, we bring all aspects of ourselves to work. In some instances, people spend more time with their coworkers than they do with their own families. It's sad, but true—especially for those of us who are entrepreneurs/workaholics. The one thing we have in common, whether we are at work or at home, is we ARE all people.

## Self-Awareness

Identity is such a big part of this first chapter because if you don't know who you are, you cannot begin a journey to develop yourself. I want to show you how important the process of self-awareness is by starting to peel back the proverbial onion. Self-awareness is the basis of everything we do. We are constantly assessing and measuring before we start a new procedure or journey in life. For instance, we need to know how much gas we have in the tank in order to know how far we can drive.

In terms of self-assessment, I often focus on the F-SET framework as I have found it to be the most effective measurement tool (both through clinical research and personal experience). F-SET was developed from a significant amount of research among powerful female military leaders who unanimously suggested that leading men was easy when these females leaders acted based on four principles: (F) femininity, (S) self-efficacy, (E) emotional intelligence, and (T) teamwork. The F-SET model is a valid basis for approaching leadership as a professional woman. I often use this framework for individuals experiencing a life transition (i.e., veterans transitioning, retirement, relocation, recent unemployment, student graduation, etc.).

In terms of self-awareness, there are many measurements we could start with. I recommend starting with a tool like the F-SET Inventory, which is a premier assessment built for success in business. If you are a male reading this, please do not be discouraged, as I have also adapted the F-SET Inventory for males. At the other end of the (F) Femininity spectrum is (M) Masculinity. The tool works well for either gender, as leadership is exclusive to the individual being true to themselves.

The F-SET Inventory can be effective for males and females because the F in F-SET is a scale of authenticity. This component does not measure how much of a man or woman you are; rather, it measures how in tune with yourself you are as a man or a woman and how that relates to your work. For instance, if you are high in femininity and you are going to be working in a steel mill, this could present some challenges for you to consider as you continue towards your work objectives.

Men and women have used the F-SET Inventory as an initial assessment to find out their areas for improvement in competencies such as Self-Efficacy, Leadership, Confidence, Emotional Intelligence, Teamwork, and Collaboration.

The best time to take it is when you are starting out on your career or life journey, and the best way to implement it is to have an expert consultant provide tailored results in alignment with your specific goals.

Only you know the details that are unique to your transformation process. If you want to know more about the F-SET Inventory assessment and leading with distinction, it can be found in the Appendix. [You can also try some other behavioral measures that give tailored feedback for your development, such as the Veteran Skills Inventory (VSI) or the Emotional Intelligence Quotient (EQi 2.0)].

## Combat Pink

Now, let me share with you a little bit about my journey. In my first co-authored book, *Leading by My Ponytail: Why Can't I Wear Pink and Be President?*, I shared my detest for *pink*... Growing up as a tomboy and loving all things opposite of pink, I never would have expected that I would write a book now talking about *embracing* my *pink* and the even-more-powerful concept of "*combat pink*." However, I recognize that *pink* is contextual and, as humans, we are complex beings. Everything we do is contextual, and I challenge you to stay with me as I use *pink* as a metaphor for the "individual" you.

I grew up in the household of a perfectionist, self-loving father and a religious, compassionate mother who could love everyone but herself. She gave everything of herself, and her only wish in life was to be a mother and wife. When my parents divorced, my siblings and I lived with our mother and visited our father every other weekend. From as early as 10 years old, I remember my father calling my mother lazy and several other names for her lack of education or ambition to match his. But despite his namecalling, my mother left the house each day to find full-time work, and she actually started her own house cleaning business to support our family.

As a ten-year-old child, I didn't understand anything about their dynamic. I remember hearing through the years all the words from my father that degraded my mother. Little did he know that I would also carry those words with me from my tiny ten-year-old mind, heart, and soul well into my adult years. "Lazy, stupid, fat, ugly…"

It led me to be a confused child growing up in a world (environment) that valued hard work and detested the perceived "laziness" of stay-at-home mothers. All of these were the ideals I grew up with and heard for many years. Despite all that, I do sincerely love my father. He was and always will be Superman, but he was wrong about my mother. My mother and I have worked on our relationship, and we have come to a place of adoration for everything she endured for and from me through the years.

I share this because you too may be that child who is now a budding young adult, or an adult with a budding young child inside you who doesn't think she/he is beautiful, or smart, or capable. This budding child might call herself/himself lazy and stupid because for years you too heard these things and held them inside your tiny mind, heart, and soul. My father's words held me back for years and created in me a terrible darkness of self-doubt and fear of failure that, at times, was so strong I couldn't look myself in the mirror. There is hope if you are in this same predicament. It isn't an instant recipe, and in order to resolve years of hurt, one must invest time to heal.

## Finding Beauty

The day I first knew I was beautiful came after my first deployment to Iraq. My sister worked in Los Angeles as a casting director for a small production company, and she arranged for me to be a part of a professional shoot to get my headshots done as a gift to me for having been deployed nearly nine months. I returned just before my 26th birthday, and I never wore makeup back then. I rarely smiled unless I was on the basketball court, because that was the only place I ever felt comfortable and pure joy.

Karen Walker, 2003

I remember getting all "dolled" up and dressing in some strange clothing, since it was considered a *high-end fashion* shoot. In walked a Bollywood actor who happened to be shooting on the set that day with some actual models, and he began selecting the models for his shoot. I remember he pointed specifically to me and said, "I would like to shoot with her, alone."

I laughed and looked around, thinking he must surely be talking about someone else. But his agent quickly came over to my sister and requested that I join the shoot. My sister, who understood the business, did some negotiating and the next thing I knew I was a part of a full-day shoot. I changed outfits multiple times and I ended up modeling for the next couple of years. I did mostly print media and some film extra work, but that day was the first time I saw a photo of me that my own parents didn't recognize me. It was the first day I knew I was beautiful.

## Acceptance and Feedback

During this time, I was slowly coming to terms with my *pink* side and understanding that being beautiful was a part of me. It didn't make me *weaker*; instead, it helped me reflect on all of those other self-doubts I had for years. Self-reflection is a double-edged sword. It can be helpful, and it can be a downright pain in the backside. You have to be willing to shine a light into some dark caverns of your life, overturn some rocks, and look around some sharp corners. You also need to listen to constructive feedback and be willing to develop yourself in areas where you fear developing.

For example, I understand through self-reflection that I can benefit from more emotional expression. Personally, it is more comfortable for me to work with numbers and facts, but when I'm working with others, I can't just spout out the most recent fact or spreadsheet to get my point across. That is a surefire way to run off everyone because most people find it boring. It isn't easy, but I found that it is more productive to my relationships to build conversations based on emotion and feeling with less data. I have really worked on my empathy skills, and it has helped me tremendously with my friendships.

I have taken several self-awareness assessments, and I can understand the trepidations around them. In fact, I develop them for a living. I live and breathe in this world. I often build and interpret measurement tools for organizations and individuals as an industrial/organizational psychologist. They really are worth the work on the user end and the business side.

When we are participating in self-reflection or self-awareness measures, it is important to consider not only our own perceptions, but also other's perceptions as well. Other's perceptions, in combination with ours, are perhaps the most helpful when you can get someone to give you their honest feedback. If in your self-report you are a great communicator, for instance, and others say that you are a mediocre communicator, that would be considered a blind spot for you. This means that others rated you lower than you rated yourself, which is an indication that this would be an area for you to explore further. Of course, this is a simplified example of self-reflection.

The real power behind figuring out "who you are" comes from gaining clarity into how you perceive the world. This is a deeper insight than you can glean from a standardized test such as the Myers-Briggs Personality Type Indicator (MBTI) assessment. This is why you need a more contextual assessment, like the F-SET Inventory assessment that I mentioned previously.

The MBTI assessment was first designed in 1943 by two psychologists (a mother and daughter), and it was not intended to be used in the workplace. It was made as a dating instrument, yet it is one of the most widely accepted personality tools used across all industries. It merely scratches the surface of personality, but thousands of organizations use it because of its familiarity. It starts a conversation about self-awareness and allows us to learn about the challenges and strengths we have, so we can grow. For those who are curious, I've been labeled an "INTJ" type on the Myers-Briggs assessment. This means I make lists for everything, organize the heck out of random things like the colors of clothes in my closet, and rather enjoy a quiet evening when no one is talking at all. I'm not quite sure how you want to use this knowledge other than a conversation starter, and that is how the MBTI gets dubbed as "standardized," in my opinion.

Yet as humans, we are not *standardized;* we are quite jagged. This means it takes many tools to measure us, and if the results are taken out of context, we can become unhinged. For example, in a library you may be comfortably quiet, but in a supermarket, you may like to sing along happily to a song you overhear playing through the speakers. Are you an introvert or an extrovert?

Therefore, it is best to take what we know about humans as *jagged* individuals and tie it to contextual measurable items called "competencies." Competencies are the knowledge, skills, abilities, and behaviors that contribute to individual and organizational performance. When we dive deeper into development areas that are linked to job competencies, we are able to practice our new-found awareness more often and, in many cases, we begin to heal ourselves in monumental ways.

You might think I am making a giant leap here from work to home-life. How can self-awareness and job competencies possibly help us heal? The answer is simple: if we can understand the whole picture of how we work and perform, then we can understand how others do, too—and as a result, we also learn how to build and maintain relationships. Furthermore, think of how much time we spend at work, or how much time our children spend at school? We spend so much time at work and at school that these important relationships often impact us when we are at home, or in a new environment (such as learning to cope with a new lifestyle of loneliness).

Since 1999, the suicide rate has increased 33% and my hypothesis is that we are living in a world of growing loneliness. By learning more about ourselves, we become healthier individuals and we can be more comfortable in our own skin. Self-awareness is a lifelong process. The process helps us grow as individuals and helps us build acceptance in our relationships. We can learn coping strategies to help break down the defense mechanisms we have been using to protect ourselves when we experience significant emotional events.

In some cases, our coping strategies can be healthy or unhealthy. We can get into the habit of doing something simply because that's the way we've always done it. We also get coping skills and defense mechanisms that have been passed down from our family or other household members. For example, your brother or sister might have called you names and your parents told you to ignore them. When someone bothers you now, your coping skill is to use the silent treatment. This may be helpful in some instances, but other times it takes your voice out of the conversation completely and leaves the other person wondering what you are thinking. They also have the opportunity to make up their own version of your story in their heads. This is how a lot of miscommunication starts—through non-communication.

After I adopted my son, I read everything I could get my hands on about adoptive parenting. I learned a lot about my own defense mechanisms around rejection as I became an adoptive parent. As I tried to cope with my son's fears of rejection, I was also dealing with my own. I worried he would reject me just as much as he worried that I would reject him. My healthy coping skills are exercising and studying/reading/writing, and I did a lot of both!

I read and I read and I read everything about adoptive parenting and single moms raising sons. All my reading paid off, as I also applied it with exercise and playtime with my son at the park almost every day. When we weren't at the park or playing hide-and-seek in the house, I was extra careful about speaking positively about my son's birth parents because all the books say it plays a huge role in the identity of the child. If I were to speak terribly about his birth mother and father, then what would he think of himself, the child who came from the union of these two individuals? I tried hard to instill positive words around my son's biological parents because I wanted to avoid him making up a story about what went unspoken. I used to worry: what if he thought I couldn't possibly see any good in him because of his upbringing? That is what every person told him before he came to me.

I feel wonderful when I hear my son say things like: "I love my smile." Or: "I love my curly hair." These are comments that I know when he first came to me he would not have said because he didn't know how to speak the unspoken and unknown, but I'm glad we both learned. He can be proud of his heritage and love himself.

Unfortunately, many times, regardless if we were raised by our biological parents or if we were adopted, we tend to fall victim to the negative language and actions that our parents inherited from their own childhoods. It is very common because we carry so much of our biological parents with us, regardless of who has raised us.

For example, sayings like "you look stupid when you make that face," "ladies don't sit like that," "men don't cry," "girls don't sweat," and so on. How you came to be who you are may be the result of subtle or unspoken rules from decades of unintended hurts. This may be why you feel cognitive dissonance over your identity, your femininity, your sexuality, or your lifestyle in general.

Cognitive dissonance occurs when you experience strong mental discomfort or "psychological stress" from simultaneously holding two or more contradictory beliefs, ideas, or values. It keeps you awake at night. It keeps you frozen from moving in the day. It can make you run from responsibility or hide from necessity. Cognitive dissonance is deeply rooted and takes a healing of sorts to uncover, investigate, remove, and unpack.

## Healing Steps

What has been so incredibly eye-opening to me about parenting has been God's gift through it all: my own healing and self-reflection. These gifts for me came much more often after the age of forty—so much so that I would become so overwhelmed I would have to take what I call "mommy timeouts." A "mommy timeout" is where mom goes into a safe location to be alone for 5–25 minutes without the kids.

Through my son's defense mechanisms from his prior years of severe neglect and abuse, I realized that I too had unhealthy coping skills as an adult that I gleaned from my own life experiences. I was now forced to practice healthy skills for both of us. Sometimes, these are known as "triggers" or "stuck points" in therapy. You will know it when you hit one in your life because it is either shooting you off like a rocket or holding you in one spot like flypaper.

For example, one of my trigger words is "lazy" and one of my stuck points is being a "failure." I know if someone (including my wonderful son) calls me "lazy" it will make me want to defend my territory and everything I believe in. But now, instead of reacting, I use a "mommy-timeout" and reflect on that because, clearly, I'm not "lazy." This is a teaching moment. Teaching in our house also means "discipline." Discipline is *not* punishment. Discipline is a great opportunity to teach. It is a parent's right and responsibility to discipline their children. Likewise, as a parent, I have had to discipline myself with a "mommy-timeout" in order to teach myself a healthy way to cope in the moment.

These stuck-point moments are mostly internal. Stuck points, remember, are the ones that are like flypaper or quicksand. My stuck point is the big "F" word… the one you can say in public. "Failure." It is an internal stuck point that I get jammed on from time to time, and I have to process through it using healthy coping mechanisms. I can tell you what works for me will not work for you because we are *jagged* individuals. To get past my stuck point, I use a simple phrase: "I have never been fired." Many times, to move past a stuck point, you must challenge it with an actual fact. Challenge your stuck points with facts. Facts help to combat the way we think in order to change the way we feel and, ultimately, the way we behave. Remember, everyone is different.

My self-awareness continues to grow daily. My own coping skills and continuous wrestling with defense mechanisms have allowed me to help others be successful as well.

One day, while talking to my mother on the phone, I heard her carry on the same way she had for as long as I have been alive. She talked about how she didn't like the way she looked in a picture I took of her. I remember my mother would often say things about herself like, "I'm so ugly in that picture," or "I'm stupid," or "I'm so fat."

But this time I spoke and said, "Don't talk about my mom like that!"

At first, she laughed but then she said, "Ok, you're right. She's not so bad, huh?"

We had a good laugh, and now when I say these types of things to my mom, it makes her smile. I like to think that she is starting to see herself a bit differently when we are together. One thing I know for sure is when she smiles and laughs, it helps me see myself differently, too. My consciousness about my mom's beauty has allowed me to accept my own beauty and strength in *pink*.

## Ductos Exemplo

This is a Latin phrase that means: *lead by example*. I am a big believer in walking the talk. It is a huge part of gaining trust and earning respect. As you continue on in this book, you will come across the secrets to *what it takes to be the best boss ever* from real-life experiences and interviews with top leaders around the world. These are a compilation of competencies (skillsets) that you can develop through practical exercises. In each chapter, I have given behavioral exercises to assist you with making great strides in development.

Good luck and *ductos exemplo.*

# CHAPTER 2

# Know Thy Self–Who Are You?

IT'S AN AGE-OLD QUESTION: WHO AM I? This isn't answered in a day or by taking the latest online personality test. You can't find out you're an *INTJ* (Myers-Briggs Trait Indicator, MBTI-reference) and then plan your life accordingly. Self-awareness is about two key aspects: awareness and development/management.

The reality is we are not in this world alone (even though the introverts would be energized by the thought of some quality alone time). It is important for us to learn about ourselves and then learn how to *manage* that knowledge within our relationships. That is a key aspect of leadership.

Leadership is about the ability to influence. In order to influence the people around you, you need to know yourself and others. My first recommendation when working with any client, counsultant, leader, or organization is to assess where you are up front. You have to know where you are starting from in order to know where you are going.

In the military, I was assigned many projects in which I was dubbed the officer-in-charge (OIC). The job of the OIC came with the same requirement of assessment/measurement. I needed to start the project knowing what shape we were in before developing a plan of action. As the training officer I would ask the office, "Where do we stand?" We would start with an internal audit. Did we have all the equipment we were supposed to have? Did we have all the required manuals and classes completed within the allotted time period? If not, I developed a plan/timeline to get our organization on track for completion.

Self-awareness is very similar. Even though talking about yourself as a "project" might make people look at you funny, the basic process is very similar. To perform an internal audit of sorts, you will need to use an assessment for your starting point. I recommend choosing a behaviorally-based assessment.

Remember, I am an industrial/organizational psychologist, so I am inclined to measure behaviors. This is the preferred approach for actually changing behaviors. Behaviorally-based assessments that I like to work with include the F-SET Inventory (F-SET), Veteran Skills Inventory (VSI), Emotional Intelligence Quotient 2.0 (EQi 2.0), Strengths Finder-Gallup, and Hogan Assessments.

When shopping around for a self-assessment, you want to choose one that offers tailored feedback results. This will prevent you from getting feedback in a pre-scripted pie chart. If your results are tailored in a one-on-one approach, you can receive feedback from a trained professional in the assessment you have taken and together you can work on possible development/management goals that align with your specific needs.

Pretty graphs and cartoon characters are great , but if you can't apply the feedback to your everyday life and relationships, it isn't self-awareness. Remember, self-awareness has a dual mission: awareness and development. To be meaningful, self-awareness must include some sort of practical application.

At the end of each chapter in this book, there will be an opportunity for you to apply what you have learned in a practical way and build this new information into habits. A big part of measuring behaviors is to be able to see where you can make the changes or improvements that are most applicable for your life. Once you identify these areas, you will be able to build the best plan to practice new behaviors. Each chapter will allow you to explore these behavioral changes in a hands-on way towards finding out *what it takes to be the best boss ever*.

## PRACTICAL APPLICATION

1. Take a self-assessment of your choice.* Be sure to choose one that looks at competencies or skillsets that are applicable to your job or leadership.

2. From your tailored feedback results, choose one item from your strengths and one item from a focus area for improvement.

3. Choose a workplace example and a home-life example for each of the items you chose in #2. Try to incorporate positive changes in these areas. Set a goal date of 60 days and write down how you will accomplish each.

*See Appendix for Assessments*

# CHAPTER 3

# Love and Resiliency

WHEN I AM CONSULTING AS AN ORGANIZATIONAL psychologist and I first mention love and leadership I get strange looks. This was also particularly true for the majority of my career, where I was often the only woman in a group of all men! Love is a deep concept, and I have written about what a leader's love entails. Others have captured it as something very selfless or even described it as "servant leadership."

I remember as an officer in the Marine Corps, we trained very hard so that one day we would have the honor and privilege to stand before our own company of Marines. Every officer trains to lead Marines, and your Marines are everything to you. They eat before you, sleep before you, shower before you. You give them everything, even if it means you have nothing. Because of this deep commitment, you know those same Marines will follow you into danger without blinking an eye.

The only way I can describe that kind of leadership is love. A love that protects, honors, commits, and lasts much like a parental relationship. Other examples I have collected from interviews about leadership love have included the relationships that leaders take the time to build with their people.

If the theme of Chapter 2 was knowing yourself, then the theme of Chapter 3 is knowing your people. The "Best Bosses" take the time to truly know their people. What are their strengths? What are their dreams, their deepest desires and fears? What are their insecurities? Who are they? Where did they grow up? What do they like to eat? What is their family like?

These leaders don't have to ask these questions because they have put in the time with their people to build a relationship where this type of information is freely shared. How is this possible? It is a conversation—and a somewhat vulnerable one at that.

Leaders are vulnerable because they are resilient. They have learned from their mistakes. When a leader is able to relate with people and show their human side, it resonates with the people they are leading. It builds authenticity, integrity, and a genuine bond.

Some of the earliest theories of personality stem from assimilation, which is how we learn our behaviors in child development from watching others. However, this type of behavior is not exclusive to children. As adults, we use assimilation and accommodation to categorize information in our minds. When we add to existing information, it is called assimilation. For instance, we work with someone and we think they are nice, and then we witness them sharing their lunch with another person. This endorses our "friendly" beliefs. Conversely, is if we believe the person is kind and we see the person take someone else's lunch when they are not looking, we will need to "accommodate" this characteristic of them with what we know of the person.

Imagine how difficult this can be if we are naturally perfectionists. We cannot bear to accept a flaw in ourselves and therefore would not be vulnerable enough to let anyone else see our true selves. It makes it almost impossible to let others get close to us and *assimilate*. It leaves them to guess or *accommodate* information about us, and in many cases, it leads them to make assumptions about our character.

When I first walk into a room, there are a lot of assumptions that happen. Let me paint a picture. First, I am five-feet five-inches tall and built like a basketball point guard with an athletically feminine frame. When I start to speak, I have a soft-spoken tone. I know right off the bat that there are so many things going through the audience's head. In 2008, I made the decision to leave active duty and go into the Reserve Forces to use my PhD. I had already completed three tours in Iraq, and everyone told me I would have no problems finding a job. After all, I was a Major-select in the Marine Corps with a PhD!

But for nearly a year, I struggled to find full-time

employment. I submitted over 10 job applications a day and drove to multiple job fairs each week. Every time, I came back empty-handed and even more deflated than when I left the house. I became so depressed that I started to really loathe my very being. I had zero self-confidence and I felt I had no self-worth. This was a very low point in my life. I start every one of my motivational speeches with this story because it is by far the most *vulnerable* moment in my life. This was a moment when I used to pray to God each night that I wouldn't wake up each morning. If you have been there, you know the feeling. I felt my life was a miserable, depressing wreck that year.

Please take heart that these feelings are fleeting, and time does pass. God hears other's prayers for us, and I thank him for His plans that only He has brilliantly for each of us.

> *"For I know the plans I have for you," declares the Lord, "plans to prosper you and not to harm you, plans to give you hope and a future."*
> —JEREMIAH 29:11

I was eventually able to climb out of where I was and I started rebuilding my confidence again, but I couldn't do it all by myself. It starts with vulnerability. By letting people know that I too had faults or chinks in my armor, I was able to see the light again and start learning how to find my passion in life.

## Building Relationships

It can be scary to build relationships. As a Marine officer going through training, I remember being told things like: "Officers don't sit." "Officers don't put their hands in their pockets." "Officers don't chew gum." "Officers don't yell."

All of this combined with my ideals from childhood led me to have a supreme perfectionist image of "Major Walker." This was at the same time when I made the switch from active duty to reservist. As I mentioned earlier, I was also struggling for nearly a year to find full-time employment, which was sucking me into a terrible depression. I couldn't look at myself in the mirror, and I found it near impossible to consider "Dr. Walker" and "Major Walker" to be the same person. I was experiencing cognitive dissonance every time I talked about the military. Who was I now?

I struggled with this identity crisis because in my eyes "Major Walker" was perfection, whereas "Dr. Walker" was studious and fun to be around. I worked to build relationships as "Dr. Walker" and slowly shared parts of "Major Walker" in order to merge my worlds. Soon I realized that when I was true to myself and letting people see the whole me—the struggles and the successes—it showed them I was relatable. It helped me to see my own resiliency. Believe it or not, it helped "Major Walker" become "Lieutenant Colonel Walker." Now "Lieutenant Colonel Walker" is also "Dr. Walker," both of whom are fun-loving, smart, wonderful people and are very much worth getting to know (although they are not perfect!).

Perfectionism truly hurts intimacy. This is a very big deal when it comes to the amount of time that leaders spend with their people, which gives a lot of weight to the saying "time is money" and "takes one to know one." Leaders who can assimilate with their people, spend time with them, and know where they come from come across as more genuine and understanding.

It can really bridge a gap in a relationship by simply sharing an element of humanity. If someone is in a painful or embarrassing moment, a leader can show true empathy by merely sitting in the moment of misery or embarrassment with that person.

I had a coworker whose son was murdered and it left a hole in her heart. It left a gaping hole in our office, too. The silence was terrible, and no one knew what to say or do. Our office was broken emotionally and functionally. Our leader at the time brought us together and shared a story with us about when he lost a dear friend to suicide. He shared with us how much it helped him to hear happy memories of his friend and not just pretend that he ever existed. This was an extremely vulnerable moment for our leader to share, but it showed his love for our office and our colleague, and it brought us closer together for the days to come because we could talk more openly together.

Sharing your sincerity for others by investing in getting to know them is a step in the right direction toward finding *what it takes to be the best boss ever.*

# PRACTICAL APPLICATION

1. Think about the two closest people to you in your life at work and outside of work.

2. Brainstorm what you know about these people. Take notes of the similarities and differences.

3. What vulnerable conversations might you be avoiding that could help you build stronger relationships with each of these people? Consider sharing a new conversation topic in the next 30 days.

# CHAPTER 4

# Problem-Solving and Conflict Resolution

CONFLICT MAKES MY STOMACH HURT!!! So how can it be a part of leadership? Healthy conflict actually exists in every group dynamic. According to hundreds of leadership interviews I have conducted, leaders who are able to problem-solve and use conflict resolution strategies are most memorable as the best bosses.

Problem-solving is a unique skillset. Another reason why self-assessment is so important is because you find out if you have a natural ability to problem-solve or if this is something you will need to outsource. Bringing in extra resources to problem-solve is actually quite common, and it's a good step to take when time permits.

Some of the best decision-making and problem-solving have resulted from inclusive techniques. For example, if hiring a new first-line supervisor, you might consider using a panel of current supervisors and staff to review and/or interview potential candidates. This gives everyone an opportunity to buy-in to the process, and it can build trust overall in the decision-making process. After a project concludes, having a "retrospective" or "after-action" inclusive meeting will allow others to provide feedback on what went well or how to improve future projects. This type of problem-solving is somewhat easier to swallow than conflict management for most people because it is more tangible and task-related.

Let's slide over to conflict resolution. This is often referred to as a "soft skill," and it is more fluid and harder to pinpoint. So, how do you know if you are good at it? Well, you must practice it. I know that is a painful answer. Conflict resolution is a lot like diversity and inclusion training. How will you react if you are faced with a discriminatory situation? You have to practice it so you know the procedures to follow in the heat of the moment. Conflict happens every day and it isn't exclusive to the workplace. So, needless to say, we have a lot of opportunities to practice.

When I worked for the Federal Aviation Administration (FAA), we provided training for conflict resolution. They referred to it as "facilitator" training for the top facility in the FAA—the Command Center. Facilitators at the Command Center needed to be able to "facilitate" conflict/conversations between multiple parties/partners.

For example, suppose that the airlines, the airport, and the Air Traffic Controllers (ATCs) have a disagreement. They need permission to fly or create a safe weather delay schedule for all of New York… Oh, and by the way, they have been fussing for 15 minutes and they needed the plan ten minutes ago!

The facilitator's job is not to solve the problem, but rather to "facilitate" the conversation between all parties. Conflict resolution is exactly that: being a very good listener, understanding each party's needs, and helping them communicate those needs to each other. As adults, we do this practically every day without realizing it. We have opportunities to listen and translate for people. I used to refer to it as helping people have "adult conversations."

Conflict resolution is often necessary when there is no longer a conversation because something has gone awry in communication that now requires you—the listener, the translator, the facilitator, the conflict resolutioner—to enter the picture (superhero music plays).

## Assuming Positive Intent

An important aspect of listening to people is being able to define the problem for them. As a facilitator, you can hear what all parties are saying and help them partner toward a resolution that meets the best interests of resolving the problem. This is part of a collaborative problem-solving and decision-making process.

A key aspect of being the best boss is self-awareness, which includes emotional intelligence. Hopefully you have had the opportunity to take a self-assessment and receive your personalized results, as problem-solving and conflict resolution is hard to do if you are unable to truly self-reflect. If we are entering into a problem or conflict the same way we always have, we will be sure to get the same results. Consider listening first and clarifying expectations when you enter into a conflict-resolution scenario or problem-solving situation. What are the expected outcomes? Who is accountable for what outcome?

Perhaps, most importantly, we should assume *positive intent* when problem-solving. In conversations, we can listen with prior baggage and hurts that determine our future behaviors/reactions. However, the best bosses assume positive intent by putting down their past experiences, old walls, and baggage so they can truly listen for new solutions. When assuming positive intent, follow-up questions are most helpful when they start with "what" and "how" instead of "why." For example: What can I do to help? How will this make us a better organization? Can you help me understand this idea?

These unique skillsets of problem-solving and conflict resolution are definitely *what it takes to be the best boss ever*.

## PRACTICAL APPLICATION

1. Practice facilitating a conversation between two friends or family members. Remember the key here is "listening" and being able to define the problem.

2. Take notes to help ensure that you listen and then repeat what each party wants.

3. Facilitate the two parties to come to a resolution. DO NOT RESOLVE THEIR PROBLEM FOR THEM. How was this experience? What was most difficult? What worked well?

# CHAPTER 5

# Recognition and Gratitude

FOR MANY ORGANIZATIONS, LEADERS BECOME LEADERS because they are the best at their job rather than because they are the best at "leading others." However, it is a catch 22, because a leader often needs knowledge of their trade AND knowledge of leading people in order to be the best boss ever. Being good at your job is a necessity. Now let's take this into context. There are some individuals put into roles that they know nothing about and become superior leaders nonetheless. Why is this significant? Because they are still good at their job—being an influential leader! They are instilling the qualities the organization needs to be successful by leading by example.

For instance, I remember a new manager at the Navy Command who was fresh out of school but accepted by everyone. He was always the first one in the office, always said good morning, asked if anyone needed help, and said thank you. When he needed to learn things about the office, he relied on his senior enlisted personnel to guide him. He also was sure to recognize them at staff meetings, gatherings, or all-hands meetings. Recognition can go a long way. When the boss knows your name (for good reasons), it can be inspiring. More importantly, a genuine by-name recognition for a job well done is encouraging that one's work isn't taken for granted.

Another significant aspect of rewards and recognition is timeliness. Timely recognition is necessary and sincere. Even though bureaucracies and processes can bog down our acts of gratitude, we can still be *the best boss ever* by being deliberate with timely recognition.

Many times, monetary rewards for employees can take several pay periods to kick into an employee's paycheck. By the time the employee sees an incentive award in their bank account, they are left wondering if there was a clerical error that they will have to pay back in the future. Instead, it is more impactful if an employee is informed that they will be receiving an incentive award prior to receiving it into their bank account. This personal recognition is a sign of gratitude and demonstrates the significance of the employee-employer relationship.

## Intrinsic Motivators

When it comes to motivational theories, people are most familiar with Maslow's hierarchy of needs that introduced the concept of intrinsic motivators as a humanistic approach for individuals. As a refresher, Maslow's hierarchy of needs is often displayed in a pyramid representing humanistic motivational needs from lowest to highest: physiological, safety, love/belonging, esteem, and self-actualization.

The need for esteem focuses on our internal need for recognition, respect, consideration, and achievement. As humans, we have a need for esteem that is driven by prestige and a feeling of personal accomplishment. Maslow's theory was that recognition of this esteem need was as important to our psychological wellbeing as our basic needs such as food, shelter, and water.

With that in mind, it really puts concepts like politeness and common courtesies into a whole new perspective. Politeness can go a long way. A simple greeting of the day (i.e., good morning, good afternoon) or please and thank you leaves a lasting memory. Failing to offer such pleasantries can leave a huge black hole.

One employee recalled how she and her boss were the only ones in the office by 6:30 a.m. every morning for three years before he retired, and he never once told her good morning. Now that's a lasting memory—OUCH!! It is extremely hard to fix that later in life. We have to consider the bridges that we build and, in some cases, the damage we do along the way.

Another employee recalled how her boss always took the time to say "Have a good weekend" every Friday for four years. Little things can make a big difference in someone's world.

As a young Captain in the Marine Corps, I worried that I couldn't be myself around my Marines. I remember seeing another female officer, a Marine Colonel, who was giving her Marines hugs as she passed out awards. I thought to myself I could never do that. I thought that if I showed any emotion, I would be seen as weak.

But as I watched more closely, I saw how she was being her true authentic self. Her Marines actually embraced her and then came to attention and saluted her with love and respect. I wondered if I would have judged her the same way if she were a male Colonel hugging his Marines? Such brotherhood, such strength. A genuine heart.

After that, I started to open up more to my Marines, letting them know what made me most proud or disappointed, or what encouraged me or distressed me as a mentor. This wasn't a therapy session with my Marines, and it doesn't need to be one with your employees, either. It is, however, an opportunity for leaders to be authentic and grateful for who they are by recognizing genuine moments in life with others.

True recognition of hard work can be exactly *what it takes to be the best boss ever*.

## PRACTICAL APPLICATION

1.  Think of the people you work most closely with and choose three of those people. What about those individuals closely matches or impacts you (positively) in a similar way?

2.  When was the last time you recognized the positive impact they had on your work/life?

3.  Write down two ways for all three people that have impacted you in a positive way in the form of a thank you note. Give it to them.

# CHAPTER 6:

# Collaboration and Trust

THIS CHAPTER COULD HAVE BEEN A WHOLE BOOK by itself, so I will try to summarize the key points for each concept. When I talk about collaboration, people automatically think of teamwork, but as we proceed, I want you to dissect these two concepts in your mind.

The way I look at teamwork is more of a close relationship for a designated result. Teamwork consisting of one-on-one friendships or "besties" is another good example of this. Teamwork is also much more task-oriented and is generally easier for most people to conceptualize. When we think of leaders and teamwork, we picture the leader influencing the team in some way. This is true, but I would say from all of my interviews that this is an *average* boss.

The *best boss* distinction comes from a boss who can collaborate and build trust. So how is collaboration different than teamwork?

Imagine collaboration more like a neighborhood where if you stretched your arms out wide you could touch neighbors in every direction. Collaboration is about building networks, building relationships. It is necessary to understand the importance of going beyond working together in one-on-one situations. Collaborative bosses stretch past their comfort zones and reach out into metaphorical neighborhoods to build relationships.

The frustrating thing about collaboration for most people is that it often has no task in mind other than to build relationships. When groups are collaborating, they may not, in a sense, "accomplish" a set objective other than simply meeting. For most type "A" personalities or go-getters, it is hard to go to a meeting to just "meet." It feels like a waste of time.

However, the building of key relationships and networks is how we allow bigger projects to get completed. If we can come to the table and have conversations to build partnerships with our neighbors, we can move the entire city.

## Common Interests

While working in the FAA, I learned a lot about the beauty of collaboration from the National Air Traffic Controllers Association (NATCA), which is the bargaining union for air traffic controllers. It was my pleasure and honor working as an organizational psychologist within the FAA, traveling throughout the Air Traffic Organization's (ATO) facilities and measuring the growth of collaboration between labor and management leadership. The two biggest steps to collaboration and trust for labor and management leadership were "defining the problem" and "sharing common interests." Finding common ground on any issue started with a relationship; by utilizing 'we' language, the two parties could define the problem and focus on providing solutions/outcomes using common interests.

One of the ways a leader shows they are a collaborative partner is in the type of language they use in the organization. A big indicator of collaboration is "we" language versus "I" language. Leadership that is willing to be conscious of these nuances is quite perceptive of the collaborative culture they are instilling. Be aware if your organization is using "us" versus "them" language; pay attention if they talk about projects and tasks in a more collaborative style using "we" and "our" more positively.

Collaborative leadership styles allow for a much more trusting work environment. Collaborative leaders do not seek to control, but rather seek to inspire others and work together as a team. Because of this openness, information is shared more freely across the organization. These free-flowing information streams cut down on silos and help facilitate better decision-making, improve agility, and create an atmosphere of trust and collaboration.

The interesting part about collaborative workspaces is the relationships and networks that are built. Highly collaborative workplaces can also be strongly integrated networks. As a new leader or coworker entering such an environment, it can be tricky to navigate these networks.

In strong integrated networks, there are attributes leaders must possess like a sense of diplomacy, a willingness to relinquish control, and a humility that moves the group towards a collaborative way of working. By encouraging individuals at all levels to take initiative and act in a manner that contributes to achieving the overall vision of the organization, one can be an inclusive and effective leader. There is such power in recognizing that everyone on the team has a voice, and this recognition also builds trust in leadership.

Capitalizing on elements of collaboration and network-building helps to build trust and increase insight into *what it takes to be the best boss ever.*

# PRACTICAL APPLICATION

1. Brainstorm about your current team or workgroup. If you are not part of a team or workgroup, consider a team you have been a part of in the past.

2. What worked well? What was most difficult? Write down three things that you could have done differently on the team.

3. Consider how the team could get the best out of you? How could they get the worst out of you? When considering your next collaborative workgroup, be sure to communicate your expectations with the team for your full buy-in (participation) in order to encourage healthy, trusting relationships from the start.

## CHAPTER 7

# Autonomy and Empowerment

WE ARE GETTING TO THE TOP STRATEGIES for *what it takes to be the best boss ever*. One of the most popular answers that I get when I ask people about the qualities of the best bosses is a boss who does NOT micromanage them and does NOT talk down to them.

The best bosses always encourage autonomy. Autonomy is the ability of employees to control their own work situation. If you have ever had the opportunity to be encouraged in this type of work environment, it makes it hard to go back to a more authoritative workplace where the leadership is constantly watching your every move.

This type of directive leadership style is rarely necessary unless you find yourself in a high-stakes, life-or-death situation (perhaps in a fire or an "active shooter" scenario). You might understand how you would need to do exactly as you are told—"Get Down!" or "Put your hands up!"

Even thinking about those types of scenarios will make anyone's heart race. However, we shouldn't need to have authoritative micromanaging instructions in our everyday jobs. This type of criterion often cripples our decision-making and leads us to be really unhappy.

The best bosses give encouragement and empowerment to their people through autonomy. It can be incredibly empowering to be able to set goals and have a feeling of choice in your work. Often the key to happiness and job satisfaction isn't more money, but autonomy and the freedom to control one's work situation.

This type of empowerment at work is an outside-the-typical-box way of thinking. I can recall one time when I was having an end-of-the-year evaluation with a supervisor and he was asking me how I could best reach my professional goals for the year. One of my goals was to write a technical report on some of my latest research and findings. I was stuck in the traditional mindset of hoping he would approve and give me more time to write during my allotted schedule.

I was shocked and speechless when my boss asked me what I needed? He suggested a writer's retreat or access to a cabin or secluded quiet area. He was truly listening and genuinely interested in my professional development. I didn't end up going to a different location, but this made him one of the best bosses I ever had.

# Thrive

I worked as a Personnel Research Psychologist for the Department of the Navy in 2010-2013, and it was a crucial time in history in terms of Department of Defense employment laws. During these years, gays and lesbians could now openly serve in the military as 'Don't Ask, Don't Tell' (DADT) was repealed and the ban on women serving in combat arms Military Occupational Specialties (MOSs) was also lifted. The key to both of these actions was a true realization that whether or not one can function in a job should be dependent on your ability to actually execute the functions of the job.

The important part about equalizing the workforce billets was providing an empowering working environment for both women and the LGBT community. Corporations and government in general have warmed up to developing affinity groups that empower specific communities and diverse groups (e.g., veterans, women, Black, Hispanic, etc.).

Research, academia, and practitioners agree that introducing minority groups in "threes" is most beneficial for growth and development. For example, in a submarine unit newly open to having women on-board, it is best to have a minimum of three women assigned to a previously all-male unit, with at least one of the three women in a leadership position. This rule of three cuts down on competition amongst the women and builds mentorship relationships while simultaneously deterring a "lone-wolf" syndrome.

## Self-Compassion

With more autonomy from a boss comes less authority and more empowerment. The beauty of this is that employees can start to feel re-charged and energized. Leadership is a continuous journey, and it is important to cultivate the ability to follow the ebb and flow. Taking constructive criticism but also being able to take the compliments that come your way as a leader are important for growth as an individual and as a team.

It can be hard for me to accept compliments at times, and even harder for me to have compassion for myself when I am struggling. With self-compassion, we give ourselves the same kindness and care that we would give to a good friend. The concept of self-compassion has been well-researched and measured by Kristin Neff, PhD. The benefits of it are truly endless and have changed the game of traditional self-talk strategies, like telling yourself to "suck it up."

Using self-compassion encourages me to actually take the time to comfort myself and care for myself in the moment. Self-compassion is more about self-kindness and less about self-judgment. I am able to use mindfulness techniques to balance out my approaches to coping with difficult everyday challenges in the heat of the moment. For instance, I can stop and tell myself, "This is really difficult right now" and "How can I comfort myself in this moment?" This approach gives me a feeling of control over my situation and helps me feel more connected with humanity rather than isolated and judged for how I'm feeling on any given day.

I encourage you to give yourself the same opportunities to enjoy every moment as a leader and celebrate the imperfections we have in life. For example, I understand I am a strong beautiful woman, except when I'm not. What that means is that I have self-compassion and understanding that I am not perfect, and I do not hold myself to the expectation of such. I want to enjoy every moment and embrace the imperfections I have. Some days will be great, some days will be hard, and some days will be downright awful.

Regardless of the type of day you are having, remember (for you and those around you) that having self-compassion will enable you to be more autonomous and actualize *what it takes to be the best boss ever*.

## PRACTICAL APPLICATION

1. Consider your latest group work scenarios, both at work and socially. When are you happiest and most comfortable?

2. What are the dynamics within these groups? How do you fit into the dynamics? How can the rule of "three" be implemented in your group work? Which one of the "three" could you be (e.g., leader, mentor, mentee)?

3. Combine your responses from #1 and #2 to create an autonomous and empowering group list. You should now see a list of tasks and a list of social dynamics. Are these in alignment? If not, how can you be more in alignment with the types of workgroups you either work with or socially engage with?

   *For example:*

   **List 1:** happiest with party-planning groups.

   **List 2:** small groups (5 people) mostly non-supervisors and women, white, I am a mentee. Examine the make-up of the group and the alignment of your goals. If you are constantly in the same groups, you will constantly be doing the same tasks with the same people.

# CHAPTER 8

# Loyalty and Integrity

THE MOST INTIMATE PART ABOUT MY JOB as an organizational psychologist can be working with people in their most vulnerable moments as I am presenting their assessment results for personal self-awareness. During this process, I am able to deliver their personalized results in a setting that is safe and dependable for them to express themselves freely and to collaborate on some developmental goals for the future.

These moments of vulnerability are golden opportunities for me to facilitate a semi-structured interview with the individual to engage and build a connection. Over the years, I have found that this semi-structured interview helps individuals to feel more of an active part of the process of enlightenment. The question that I have gleamed the most information from in all of my interviews has always been:

*Can you describe to me the best boss you ever had?*

The most universal attribute for what it takes to be the best boss I ever had is: loyalty. When I first started doing leadership development assessments and coaching, I would ask individuals this simple question.

*Can you describe to me the best boss you ever had?*

From this question, I would always be surprised to find that the answers aligned with the first answer, namely *loyalty*. They would describe this as the feeling that their bosses had their backs and their boss would stand up for them if they weren't in the room.

What an amazing feeling it is to know that someone has your back. How fascinating that people would correlate this feeling with the best and most memorable bosses they have had. This really had my human behavior curiosity meter kicking in to find out more.

I found that the stories involving loyalty and supervisors are deeply linked to integrity. By definition, loyalty means faithfulness to a cause, ideal, custom, institution, or product. When we apply loyalty to relationships, it brings in additional elements of commitment and honesty.

Here is what it comes down to if employees are expecting their managers and supervisors to be loyal:

- **Actions in the open.** If you have to hide it then it can be perceived as lying.

- **Sharing honest thoughts and feelings.** If you can't say it to their face, don't say it at all.

- **Weather the storm together.** Standing side-by-side through both the good and tough times, late nights, praises, or butt-chewings.

- **Be inclusive.** Consider others first before volunteering them for work or details.

These are some quick examples to help guide you toward building loyalty in any relationship. The best part about these quick tips is that they also help you in developing and displaying integrity.

Integrity is defined in many ways, but I think the easiest behavior-based explanation is: *walking the talk*. Do your actions support your words? When a person with a high level of integrity makes a mistake, they will genuinely apologize and you will find that they will do their best to not repeat it. It is important to them to uphold a level of good character.

## Respect

The definition of respect comes from a feeling of deep admiration for someone or something elicited by their abilities, qualities, or achievements. It is so hard to gain respect when we have lost it because of how quickly the qualities of respect can be deteriorated. Think of trust and respect like a bank account. Our actions are like daily deposits and withdrawals in this account, and when we do not reinforce positive behaviors in our relationships and organizations, we make daily withdrawals until we empty out the account.

In some cases, it takes weeks, months, or even years to earn enough positive interaction to deposit back into these respect and trust accounts. This can be scary and we might withdraw from the whole process altogether.

As leaders, it is important to recognize the anxiety we feel when we trust others through a willingness to extend trust first. This often means we need to assume positive intent and model this behavior for others in our organizations. These significant building blocks of loyalty and integrity are *what it takes to be the best boss ever.*

## PRACTICAL APPLICATION

1. Clarify expectations. Before you embark on anything new (i.e., a project, business partnership, romantic relationship, etc.), start practicing telling people what your intentions are. "Tell them what you will do, tell them what you are doing, then tell them what you did." This builds a pattern of consistency.

2. Choose an upcoming project or an event to use this strategy/approach. For one week, dedicate your efforts towards being consistent and deliberate in your message. Tell people what you are going to tell them. Then tell them. Then tell them what you told them. This deliberate approach builds integrity in your work and communication.

3. When the week is over, ask for honest feedback about your communication strategy. It is important that you listen first. Practice closing your mouth before answering and assuming positive intent in their comments. Repeat back what you have heard before you respond and be sure to thank them for the feedback. This is building a relationship that provides a safe space for feedback that will help people trust that they can return to the space in the future.

## CHAPTER 9

# Walker's Notes for What It Takes to Be the Best Boss Ever

WHAT I KNOW ABOUT THE HUMAN PSYCHE is that we remember the first and last things we read and/or see. I am sure some of you went to this chapter first instead of reading everything else, and that is exactly why I wrote this final chapter in the manner I did. I'm often asked what the interviews tell me about the attributes of the worst bosses? Can't I just be the opposite of her/him?

If only it were that easy. The problem is that we *always* ponder on the last thing we hear. It is much like a child running out the door and we shout out to them, "Don't spill anything on your new white shirt!" or "Don't text and drive!" The problem is the "Don't" is completely negated. Instead, the brain ruminates on "spill on the new white shirt" or "text and drive." This is the reason why affirmations are much more effective for reinforcing behavioral changes.

In this chapter, I am going to put a positive twist on all the worst boss behaviors I heard in the previous interviews. For example, positive spins for the previous examples would look like this: "Remember to keep your new white shirt clean" and "Remember to put your phone on safe mode when you're driving."

You can gradually celebrate success and improve upon who you are, one experience at a time. Use the tools and skills from these Walker's notes along with the chapters, assessments, and the Appendix as you incorporate *what it takes to be the best boss ever.*

## Walker's Notes for
# *WHAT IT TAKES TO BE THE BEST BOSS EVER*

- Provide employees with autonomous work whenever possible; this builds a trusting relationship.

- Assume positive intent when starting a difficult conversation, meeting, or project.

- Use inclusive language like "we" and "our" instead of "I" and "me" when talking about your organizations and teams.

- Recognize people often in a variety of ways and be grateful for feedback, positive or constructive.

- Welcome conflict as an opportunity to practice resolution through open and honest (transparent) conversations.

- Treat others like you want to be treated.

- Lead by example. Know yourself so you can be the best you can be and be open to learning about how you engage and manage with others.

- Strive to be better than the best boss you ever had through the awareness of yourself. Learn how to manage your strengths and challenges around others.

# PRACTICAL APPLICATION

1. Choose one assessment focus area that needs improvement and make it a priority for the next three days. Be deliberate in this area—where will you use this skillset? With whom? And when? Write down your plan and record your progress.

2. Choose one chapter and focus on those key skillsets for two weeks. Get feedback from a coworker, a peer, a mentor, a family member, and a child. Children can be surprising and eye-openingly honest. Remember, we can learn something from everyone. Write down the feedback you get and be sure to repeat back to each person what you heard them say to you. Follow up with them in two weeks.

3. Choose one item from Walker's notes and commit to applying it for the next thirty days. Tell someone in your life that you are making this commitment. Write it down. Set a reminder on the 30th day in your calendar to check in with the person to hold you accountable on your progress.

# Appendix

## *F-SET Inventory*

F-SET Inventory is a premier assessment tool designed to measure necessary components for both women's and men's success in business. This unique and sophisticated tool is given in combination with a personalized interview with a certified expert consultant. Each participant receives their results along with areas of opportunity for self-development and personal transformation towards their career and/or life plan. The F-SET Inventory has been used in the guidance and transformation consultation of men and women in various professions and career levels.

This tool offers the individual an opportunity to measure their skillsets with a proven model of leadership and explore avenues for development. Take your assessment in minutes and then experience your results in a confidential 60-minute consultation with one of our trained experts. The F-SET Inventory is a product of KW Productions and can be accessed at **www.kw-productions.com/tools**

### Emotional Intelligence Quotient 2.0 (EQi2.0)

The Emotional Quotient Inventory (EQi-2.0) measures emotional and social intelligence competencies. It is an excellent way to understand the competencies of the individual as well as group dynamics in order to decide your next steps to becoming a more effective leader or build a stronger team. The EQi 2.0 is a product of MHS Assessments, however KW Productions has EQi 2.0 certified experts to administer the inventory and provide detailed private individual and group consultations.

### Veteran Skills Inventory (VSI)

Veterans are highly skilled individuals competing with other job applicants every day. The Veteran Skills Inventory (VSI) allows veterans to compete when quality matters more than quantity. The VSI is a multi-faceted skills inventory for veterans to take to potential civilian employers that easily translates their competencies and ranks them on a continuum of success profiles against other successful candidates in a multitude of industries.

The VSI allows a veteran to display their competency in judgment, decision-making, problem-solving, initiative, leadership, and multiple other competencies in comparison to other job applicants in an employer's pool. The VSI is a product of KW Productions and can be accessed at www.kw-productions.com/tools

## *Leadership Realignment*

Change can be difficult in any part of our work-life balance and at any level in the organization. KW Productions utilizes Leadership Alignment Teams (LAT) to best transition the change process by working closely within the organization's leadership levels and workforce. We use a multi-faceted approach to assess organizational behaviors alongside the culture/environment in order to build a tailored intervention to move everyone forward based on your new objectives.

We are highly skilled when it comes to Labor and Management alignment or Management-only alignment settings. When your organization is changing, consider using our LATs to assist in the change process and set yourselves up for success. LATs are a product of KW Productions and can be accessed at www.kw-productions.com/tools

## *Organizational Health Gauge (OHG)*

The Organizational Health Gauge (OHG) survey measures behavioral change in your organization in four key areas that are essential for effectiveness: Communication, Collaborative Decision-Making, Leadership Alignment, and Environment/Culture. It is an online assessment tool that can be administered securely to your entire organization to help you build action plans for your leadership to strive for sustainable change.

This is the only tool that allows leaders to have an ROI on change management. Find out just how much your organization has moved the needle in 4, 6, 9, or 12 months from any change initiative. Remember, what gets measured is what gets done. The OHG is a product of KW Productions and can be accessed at www. kw-productions.com/tools

**To access any KW Production tools/consultants:**
www.kw-productions.com/tools

## BEHAVIORAL MEASUREMENT DESIGNS

There are many strengths to look for in a behavioral measurement or test design. As a basic starter test, it is important that the measurement tool has a way to study overt and observed actions. These types of scales are successful for organizational and individual development because they allow individuals to compare their actions on a range of common behaviors.

In psychological research, the most widely used self-report inventories use a *Likert scale* to assess personality, attitudes and behaviors. While these are the most common types of scales, they have their benefits and shortcomings.

*For example:* A *Likert scale* measures whether you agree or disagree with a statement or how strongly you will act in a certain situation.

## Likert Scales

*I am a very understanding person.*

| A | B | C | D | E |
|---|---|---|---|---|
| None of the time | A little of the time | Some of the time | Most of the time | All of the time |

These *Likert scales* are more traditional types of test designs, and although accurate and helpful in measuring behaviors, they also have their disadvantages. For example, due to the extreme ends of the scales (e.g., none of the time, all of the time) people can sometimes avoid using the full range of the scale. This can force scores towards the middle of the spectrum, which may make *Likert scales* less accurate than other behavioral scales.

## Other Behavioral Scales

There are a variety of behavioral rating scales that are available for use for researchers, practitioners, and clinical practice that have benefits going beyond the traditional *Likert scale*. Some of these scales are the *Forced Choice* and *Behaviorally Anchored Rating Scales* (BARS) designs. Each has several advantages, such as:

- They quantify and systematically organize client information;, administration and scoring is generally quick and easy.

- Most allow for comparison ratings across respondents and/or settings.

- They are norm-referenced instruments—the client's symptoms and behaviors can be compared with those of his or her peers.

- They are more accurate and generally less fakable.

- *Forced Choice* design is harder to guess what is being measured and what is high or low, which can also reduce faking.

- They are often more enjoyable for the test taker than *Likert scale* tests because they take less time to finish, which increases completion rates on any platform.

Sample behavioral scales are below:

### Forced Choice

*Which statement best describes you at work?*

| A | B |
|---|---|
| Sometimes anticipates difficulties | Very easy to talk to |

### Behaviorally Anchored Rating Scale (BARS)

| Novice | Advanced Beginner | Competent | Practitioner | Expert |
|---|---|---|---|---|
| I'm just starting to learn this, and I need assistance often. | I'm starting to get it, but I still need someone to coach me through it. | I can mostly accomplish it by myself, but still need other's assistance when things get difficult. | I understand it well and could thoroughly teach it to someone else. | I understand it, I can teach it to others, and I am often asked for my advice on this topic. |

# About the Author

Dr. Karen M. Walker, Lieutenant Colonel, USMC (ret.)

**Dr. Karen M. Walker** is a well-decorated retired Marine Corps officer with a distinguished military career that includes three combat deployments in support of Operation Iraqi Freedom. She is an expert in organizational psychology, an author, and an advocate for diversity and change as she strives to improve the transition experience for veterans.

Dr. Walker has an extensive background in government, corporate industries, and academia, as well as being an entrepreneur herself. Her experiences range from the Department of Defense, U.S. Secret Service, Federal Aviation Administration, Department of Housing and Urban Development, Synergy Learning Institute 501(c)(3), Final Notice Investigative Services Group, University of New Mexico, University of the Rockies, and Ashford University, along with co-authoring one of *Inc. Magazine*'s Top 60 Leadership books for women, *Leading by My Ponytail: Why Can't I Wear Pink and Be President?* and an award-winning screenplay "Battle Cries."

Dr. Walker also gives her time to many non-profit organizations that engage and enrich veteran women and their communities. In 2017, she started a professional development program for women veterans called *Combat Boots to Heels* through Synergy Learning Institute, a nonprofit vocational college. The program helps women veterans in any stage of their transition from the military, measuring where they are and helping them build a confident path towards wherever they want to be. http://www.synergylearninginstitute.org/combat-boots-to-heels/

In 2018, Dr. Karen launched her own business, KW Productions, an expansive organization offering a library of innovative tools that *predict the future*. The tools are proprietary to KW Productions, although certification and licensure for consultants who work in management consulting and similar fields are offered. KW Productions offers assessments in the area of: leadership development, organizational behaviors, climate assessments, personality measurement, and much more that enable workforce practices to be more fair, equitable, and legally defensible. www.kw-productions.com

She has been involved in various public speaking engagements, co-hosts the Empowering Your Pink Podcast (empoweringyourpink.libsyn.com), the *What's Really Going On?* show (www.kw-productions.com/blog), and has competed for over 10 years in All-Marine basketball across the nation.

Dr. Walker resides in Maryland with her spouse and three children.

To reach Dr. Karen M. Walker, LtCol, USMC (Ret.), please email: DrCombatPink@gmail.com